CFPB Dodd-Frank Mortgage Rules Readiness Guide

The Consumer Financial Protection Bureau (CFPB or Bureau) is updating the CFPB Dodd-Frank Mortgage Rules Readiness Guide (Guide) to help financial institutions come into and maintain compliance with the new mortgage rules outlined in Part I of this Guide. The CFPB has designed this Guide for use by institutions of all sizes.

This Guide summarizes the mortgage rules finalized by the CFPB as of August 1, 2014, but it is not a substitute for the rules. Only the rules and their official interpretations can provide complete and definitive information regarding their requirements. You can find these rules at http://www.consumerfinance.gov/regulatory-implementation/. Each rule description below includes a hyperlink with additional information, including Small Entity Compliance Guides, which may make the rule easier to digest.

This Guide consists of:

    Part I - Summary of the Rules

    Part II - Readiness Questionnaire

    Part III - Frequently Asked Questions

    Part IV - Tools

The questionnaire in Part II is not intended to encompass all details of a comprehensive compliance program. It is not a replacement for the examination procedures or regulations. It is intended to serve as a guide in preparing for implementation of the mortgage rules and in performing a self-assessment.

This document is available online only and is updated periodically. We invite your feedback on this guide. How useful is it in preparing for compliance with the rules? Do you have suggestions for improving it? Please send feedback to: CFPB_MortgageRulesImplementation@cfpb.gov.

If, after reviewing the resources on the CFPB Regulatory Implementation page and the related regulations and commentary, you have a question regarding regulatory interpretation; please email CFPB_reginquiries@cfpb.gov with your specific question, including reference to the applicable regulation sections.

For more information about the CFPB's supervision policies and procedures, please contact CFPB_Supervision@CFPB.gov. If your company is supervised by an agency other than the CFPB, please contact that agency with questions about supervision policies and procedures.

Part I – Summary of the Rules

Beginning in 2013, the Bureau issued several final rules concerning mortgage markets in the United States pursuant to the Dodd-Frank Wall Street Reform and Consumer Protection Act (Dodd-Frank Act), Public Law 111-203, 124 Stat. 1376 (2010). The rules amend several existing regulations, including Regulations Z, X, and B. Below are summaries related to these rules, beginning with rules required under Title XIV of the Dodd-Frank Act (Title XIV Rules) and followed by the Integrated Mortgage Disclosures under the Real Estate Settlement Procedures Act (RESPA) and the Truth in Lending Act (TILA) (collectively TILA-RESPA Integrated Disclosure rule). An overview of rule content is also available in the Small Entity Compliance Guides. (See the last page for links to these guides). The CFPB will continue to provide updates to the rules when necessary. Updates will be posted, along with a summary of the changes, on the CFPB Regulatory Implementation page.

Title XIV Rules

Ability-to-Repay and Qualified Mortgage Standards (Regulation Z)

The CFPB amended Regulation Z, which implements TILA. Before the amendments, Regulation Z, among other things, prohibited a creditor from making a higher-priced mortgage loan without regard to the consumer's ability to repay the loan. The amendments implement Sections 1411 and 1412 of the Dodd-Frank Act, which generally require creditors to make a reasonable, good faith determination of a consumer's ability to repay any consumer credit transaction secured by a dwelling (excluding an open-end credit plan, timeshare plan, reverse mortgage, or temporary loan), and establish certain protections from liability under this requirement for "Qualified Mortgages." The amendments also implement Section 1414 of the Dodd-Frank Act, which limits prepayment penalties. Finally, the amendments require creditors to retain evidence of compliance with the rule for three years after a covered loan is consummated.

The amendments were effective for transactions for which the creditor received an application on or after January 10, 2014.

Note: on July 11, 2014, the Bureau clarified that the ability to repay requirements do not apply to certain successors in interest where the transaction does not qualify as an assumption under Regulation Z.

Escrow Requirements under the Truth in Lending Act (Regulation Z)

The CFPB amended Regulation Z to implement Dodd-Frank Act changes to TILA's escrow requirements. Regulation Z already required creditors to establish escrow accounts for higher-priced mortgage loans secured by a first lien on a principal dwelling. The rule implements statutory changes made by the Dodd-Frank Act that lengthen the time required to maintain a mandatory escrow account established for a higher- priced mortgage loan to five years from one year. The rule also exempts certain transactions from the statute's escrow requirement. The primary exemption applies to mortgage transactions extended by creditors that (1) operate predominantly in rural or underserved areas for the preceding three years, (2) together with their affiliates originate a limited number of first-lien covered transactions, (3) have assets below a certain threshold adjusted annually, and (4) together with their affiliates do not maintain escrow accounts on extensions of consumer credit secured by real property or a dwelling that are currently serviced by the creditors or their affiliates (subject to certain exceptions).

The amendments were effective June 1, 2013.

High-Cost Mortgage and Homeownership Counseling (Regulations X and Z)

The CFPB amended Regulation X and Z to implement the Dodd-Frank Act's amendments to TILA and RESPA by expanding the types of mortgage loans that are subject to the protections of the Home Ownership and Equity Protection Act of 1994 (HOEPA), revising and expanding the tests for coverage under HOEPA, and imposing additional restrictions on mortgages that are covered by HOEPA, including a pre-loan counseling requirement. The amendments also impose certain other requirements related to homeownership counseling, including a requirement that consumers receive information about homeownership counseling providers. An interpretive rule provided instructions for generating a list of homeownership counseling organizations using data provided by CFPB or the Department of Housing and Urban Development.

The amendments were effective for transactions for which the creditor received an application on or after January 10, 2014.

Mortgage Servicing Rules (Regulations X and Z)

The CFPB amended Regulation X, which implements RESPA, and the official interpretation to Regulation X, as well as Regulation Z, which implements TILA, and the official interpretation to Regulation Z, to implement provisions of the Dodd-Frank Act regarding mortgage loan servicing.

Specifically, the Regulation X amendments implement Dodd-Frank Act sections addressing servicers' obligations: to correct errors asserted by mortgage loan borrowers; to provide certain information requested by such borrowers; and to provide protections to such borrowers in connection with force-placed insurance. Additionally, the amendments require servicers to establish reasonable policies and procedures to achieve certain delineated objectives; to provide information about mortgage loss mitigation options to delinquent borrowers; and to establish policies and procedures for providing delinquent borrowers with continuity of contact with servicer personnel capable of performing certain functions. The amendments establish procedures for the review of borrowers' applications for available loss mitigation options. Further, the amendments modify and streamline certain existing servicing-related provisions of Regulation X.

The amendments to Regulation Z implement Dodd-Frank Act sections addressing initial rate adjustment notices for adjustable-rate mortgages, periodic statements for residential mortgage loans, prompt crediting of mortgage payments, and responses to requests for payoff amounts. The amendments also include rules governing the scope, timing, content, and format of disclosures to consumers regarding the interest rate adjustments of their variable-rate transactions.

The amendments rules were effective January 10, 2014.

ECOA Valuations for Loans Secured by a First Lien on a Dwelling (Regulation B)

The CFPB amended Regulation B, which implements the Equal Credit Opportunity Act (ECOA), and the Bureau's official interpretations to implement the Dodd-Frank Act to ECOA concerning appraisals and other valuations. In general, the revisions to Regulation B require creditors to provide applicants with free copies of all appraisals and other written valuations developed in connection with an application for a loan to be secured by a first lien on a dwelling, and require creditors to notify applicants in writing that copies of appraisals will be provided to them promptly.

The amendments were effective for loans to be secured by first liens on dwellings for which the creditor received an application on or after January 18, 2014.

TILA Appraisals for Higher-Priced Mortgage Loans (Regulation Z)

The CFPB issued final rules to amend Regulation Z jointly with the Federal Reserve Board, FDIC, FHFA, NCUA, and OCC. This rule implements new appraisal provisions in TILA that were added by the Dodd-Frank Act. These rules require creditors to obtain a full interior appraisal by a certified or licensed appraiser for non-exempt "higher-risk mortgage loans." The Bureau applied these rules to all higher-priced mortgage loans (HPMLs). HPMLs are mortgages with annual percentage rates that exceed the average prime offer rate by a specified percentage. The rule also requires a second such appraisal at the creditor's expense for certain properties held for less than 180 days. Exemptions include qualified mortgages, reverse mortgages, bridge loans, construction loans of $25,000 or less and certain "streamlined" refinancings. Appraisal requirements for certain manufactured homes are effective on July 18, 2015. In addition, the rule requires creditors to provide the consumer with a copy of all written appraisals performed in connection with the HPML at least 3 days prior to closing.

The amendments were effective January 18, 2014.

Loan Originator Compensation Requirements (Regulation Z)

The CFPB amended Regulation Z to implement Dodd-Frank Act amendments that impose requirements and restrictions on: loan originator compensation; qualifications of, and registration or licensing of loan originators; compliance procedures for depository institutions; mandatory arbitration; and the financing of credit insurance. The amendments revise or provide additional commentary on Regulation Z's definition of a loan originator, restrictions on loan originator compensation, including prohibitions on dual compensation and compensation based on a term of a transaction or a proxy for a term of a transaction, and to recordkeeping requirements. The rule also establishes tests for when loan originators can be compensated through certain profits-based compensation arrangements. The rule did not prohibit payments to and receipt of payments by loan originators when a consumer pays upfront points or fees in the mortgage transaction. Instead the Bureau will first study how points and fees function in the market and the impact of this and other mortgage-related rulemakings on consumers' understanding of and choices with respect to points and fees.

The amendments were effective on three separate dates: the prohibition on mandatory arbitration was effective June 1, 2013; the provisions on financing credit insurance and including the loan originator's name and Nationwide Mortgage Licensing System and Registry (NMLSR) ID on loan documents were effective January 10, 2014; and the loan originator compensation provisions were effective January 1, 2014.

Policy Guidance on Supervisory and Enforcement Considerations Relevant to Mortgage Brokers Transitioning to Mini-Correspondent Lenders

The Bureau issued policy guidance on July 17, 2014, expressing its concerns about mortgage brokers that have set up arrangements with wholesale lenders in which they purport to act as mini-correspondent lenders. The policy guidance points out that the requirements and restrictions that RESPA and TILA and their implementing regulations impose on compensation paid to mortgage brokers do not depend on the labels that parties use in their transactions.

TILA-RESPA Integrated Disclosure rule

As directed by the Dodd-Frank Act, the CFPB finalized the TILA-RESPA Integrated Disclosure rule that integrates the mortgage loan disclosures required under TILA and sections 4 and 5 of RESPA. The TILA-RESPA rule contains new requirements and two disclosure forms that consumers will receive in the process of applying for and consummating a mortgage loan. The rule also explains in detail how to fill out and use the forms.

First, the **Loan Estimate** combines two existing forms, the Good Faith Estimate (GFE) and the initial Truth-in Lending disclosure (initial TIL) into one form. The **Loan Estimate** must be provided to consumers no later than the third business day after they submit a loan application. The rule defines a loan application as having six of the seven elements that RESPA required: consumer's name, consumer's income, consumer's social security number to obtain a credit report, property address, estimate of the value of the property and mortgage loan amount sought. The definition in the rule does not include RESPA's seventh, catch-all term "any other information deemed necessary by the loan originator."

Second, the **Closing Disclosure** combines two existing forms, the Settlement Statement (HUD-1) and Truth-in-Lending disclosures (final TIL) into one form. The **Closing Disclosure** must be provided to consumers at least three business days before consummation of the loan.

The forms use clear language and design to make it easier for consumers to locate key information, such as interest rate, monthly payments, and costs to close the loan. The forms also provide more information to help consumers decide whether they can afford the loan and to facilitate comparison of the cost of different loan offers, including the cost of the loans over time.

There are new tolerance levels for disclosed estimates and restrictions on fees and actions taken before the consumer has received the Loan Estimate and indicated an intent to proceed with the transaction.

The TILA-RESPA rule applies to most closed-end consumer mortgages. It does not apply to home equity lines of credit (HELOCs), reverse mortgages, or mortgages secured by a mobile home or by a dwelling that is not attached to real property. The rule also does not apply to loans made by persons who are not considered "Creditors" under TILA because they make five or fewer mortgages in a year.

Regulatory implementation support materials on the TILA-RESPA Integrated Disclosure rule can be found at http://www.consumerfinance.gov/regulatory-implementation/tila-respa/. There you will find a Compliance Guide, a Guide to Forms, Integrated loan disclosure forms & samples with blank model loan estimates and closing disclosures showing fields annotated to show rule citations, alternative loan type and Spanish language samples.

The amendments are effective for transactions for which the creditor receives an application on or after August 1, 2015.

Part II – Readiness Questionnaire

This questionnaire should be used as a self-assessment in determining your progress towards compliance with the new mortgage rules. This document is not an examination tool and will not be added to the Examination Manual; it is intended to be a voluntary guide for preparation. It can also serve as a guide for discussions with examiners. The extent of those discussions may be determined by your institution's size, products offered, risk mitigation, and overall strength of your compliance management system.

A. Developing an Implementation Plan

1. Evaluate the current products or services you offer to determine applicability:

    - Do you offer mortgage loans to consumers?

    - Do you offer any of the following mortgage products:

        - Closed-end credit secured by a dwelling?

        - Home equity lines of credit secured by a dwelling (*i.e.*, HELOCs)?

        - Mortgages that qualify as higher-priced mortgages under section 1026.35 of Regulation Z?

        - Mortgages that qualify as high-cost mortgages under section 1026.32 of Regulation Z?

        - Loans that are intended to meet the criteria for Qualified Mortgages under section 1026.43 of Regulation Z?

        - Second mortgages that meet the requirements of 1026.32 or 1026.35 of Regulation Z?

    - Do you service mortgage loans or own servicing rights?

    - Have you sold servicing rights to mortgage notes that you own?

2. Based on the products or services you offer, determine which regulatory amendments impact them.

    - What are the requirements that apply for each of your products?

- Have you obtained, reviewed, and considered the various bulletins, updates to rulemakings, and other requirements or guidance related to the final rules summarized in this Guide?

- Do you qualify for any exemptions? (Refer to the Small Entity Compliance Guides listed at the end of this document or the rules themselves for additional information on exemptions)

- Have you discussed which rules apply and any potential exemptions with your compliance counsel, as applicable, or regulator?

3. Have you developed an implementation plan?

    - Have you performed a gap analysis to determine what business, operational, and automated transaction processes need to change as a result of the new rules?

    - Has the plan been developed in consultation with or reviewed by key stakeholders, such as legal, compliance, and information technology?

    - Does it contain key milestones, dates for completion of required steps for compliance, testing plans, and progress reports?

        - How are you tracking progress?

        - Who reviews progress reports?

    - Does the plan include an audit review?

        - Have testing procedures been defined?

        - How are results and progress tracked?

    - Does the plan identify the responsible parties for developing the plan, ensuring adherence to the plan, and future compliance?

        - Is progress reported to senior management or the board (or similar oversight functions), as applicable?

    - Has the plan been approved by senior management and the board (or similar oversight functions), as appropriate?

    - Is your plan on schedule?

- If not, has the deviation from schedule been approved by the board, or similar oversight function, or senior management, as appropriate, and discussed with regulators?

- Are all aspects of your plan scheduled to be completed prior to the rules' effective dates?

- Have you discussed your implementation plan with your regulators and compliance counsel, as applicable?

    - Have discussions with regulators resulted in any changes to your implementation plan?

- Do you have contracts with any third parties related to mortgage activities?

    - If so, have you discussed and evaluated their implementation plan?

    - Do you have a back-up plan should the vendor not fully implement the necessary changes prior to the effective dates?

    - Additional questions regarding this topic can be found in the section below titled Service Provider Management

B. Policies and Procedures

1. Do your policies and procedures reflect the appropriate provisions in the following rules?

    Note: The list below does not encompass all possible provisions that may apply to your institution. For a more detailed list of all provisions, requirements, and exemptions please visit http://www.consumerfinance.gov/regulatory-implementation/

    - Ability-to-Repay and Qualified Mortgage Standards (Reg Z 1026.43)

        Ability-to-Repay

        If you will make loans that are not Qualified Mortgages, do your policies and procedures address the key components of the ability-to-repay provisions, including:

        - Obtaining and verifying certain financial information related to the consumer(s)?

- Ensuring that borrowers have sufficient assets or income to pay back the mortgage?

- For adjustable-rate mortgages, that the monthly payment is calculated using either a fully indexed rate or an introductory rate, whichever is higher?

- Any exemptions that apply and a full description of when the exemptions apply and conditions for exemptions (e.g., for a customer trying to refinance certain risky loans only after specific conditions are met)?

Qualified Mortgages

Do your policies and procedures address the key components of the qualified mortgage provisions, including:

- Documenting, where applicable, that loans were eligible for purchase or guarantee by Fannie Mae or Freddie Mac or other federal agencies, or that they were insured or guaranteed by FHA or VA?

- Restrictions on charging points and fees and prohibition of certain risky loan features (as applicable)?

- Limits on debt to income ratios (as applicable)?

- Full descriptions of qualifications for any qualified mortgage provisions (e.g., if the loan is made by a smaller creditor)?

- Escrow Requirements under TILA (Reg Z 1026.35)

Do your policies and procedures address the key components of the higher-priced mortgage loan escrow provisions, including but not limited to:

- Requirements to establish and maintain escrow accounts for at least five years after consummating a higher-priced mortgage loan?

- Whether you qualify for any exemptions and a full description why (e.g., if you are a smaller creditor operating predominantly in rural or underserved areas and meet the other elements of that exemption)?

- Limited exemptions for "common interest communities."

- High-Cost Mortgage and Homeownership Counseling (Reg Z 1026.32 and Reg X 1024.20)

    Do your policies and procedures address the key components of the High-Cost Mortgage provisions, including:

    - Identifying High-Cost mortgages under the revised HOEPA coverage tests?
        - Determining the applicable average prime offer rate.
        - Determining points and fees thresholds.
        - Determining prepayment penalty triggers.
    - Imposing limitations and restrictions on certain loan terms for HOEPA loans?

    Do your policies and procedures address the key components of the Homeownership Counseling provisions including:

    - Identifying when Homeownership Counseling is required?
    - Providing a list of homeownership counseling agencies to applicants within three business days after they apply for a federally-related mortgage loan?
    - Receiving confirmation that borrowers have received the appropriate counseling before making a high-cost loan or a loan that provides for or permits negative amortization to the borrower?

- Mortgage Servicing Rules (Regulations X and Z)

    Do your policies and procedures address the key components of the Mortgage Servicing provisions, including:

    - Periodic billing statements
    - Interest-rate adjustment notices for ARMs
    - Prompt payment crediting and payoff statements
    - Force-placed insurance
    - Error resolution and information requests

- General servicing policies, procedures, and requirements

    o Assessing and providing timely and accurate information

    o Properly evaluating loss mitigation applications

    o Facilitating oversight of, and compliance by, service providers, including attorneys handling foreclosures

    o Facilitating transfer of information during servicing transfers

    o Informing borrowers of the written error resolution and information request procedures

- Early intervention with delinquent borrowers

- Continuity of contact with delinquent borrowers

- Loss mitigation procedures

- Valuations for First Lien Loans Secured by a Dwelling (Reg B 1002.14)

Do your policies and procedures address the key components of the ECOA Valuations provisions, including:

- Notifying applicants of their right to receive copies of all valuations and appraisals developed in connection with the application, along with other information required in the notice?

- Providing applicants a copy of each appraisal and other written valuation "promptly upon their completion" or three business days prior to consummation (for closed-end credit) or account opening (for open-end credit), whichever is earlier?

- That fees cannot be charged in connection with providing a copy of the appraisal or valuation?

- Appraisals for Higher-Priced Mortgage Loans (Reg Z 1026.35)

Do your policies and procedures address the key components of the higher-priced mortgage loan appraisal provisions, including:

- For all higher-priced mortgage loans that are not eligible for at least one of the several exemptions from the rule:

- o notifying applicants of their right to receive copies of any written appraisal developed, along with other information required in the notice?

- o obtaining a written appraisal (including a physical visit of the interior of the property) performed by a certified or licensed appraiser?

- o obtaining an additional written appraisal (including a physical visit of the interior of the property), at no cost to the borrower, in connection with certain "flipped" properties?

- o providing consumer a free copy of all written appraisals for the transaction at least three business days before consummation?

- Loan Originator Compensation Requirements (Reg Z 1026.36)

Do your policies and procedures address the key components of the Loan Originator Compensation provisions, including:

- Requirements prohibiting a loan originator's compensation from being based on any of the transaction's terms?

- Requirements that your individual loan originators be licensed or registered as applicable under the Secure and Fair Enforcement for Mortgage Licensing Act of 2008 (SAFE Act) and other applicable laws?

- Requirements that your loan originators provide their name and unique identifier under the Nationwide Mortgage Licensing System and Registry on loan documents?

- Requirements for maintaining records concerning loan originator compensation for at least three years?

- Assuring that a loan originator that receives compensation directly from a consumer cannot receive compensation from another person in connection with the same transaction unless there is an exemption?

- Assuring compliance with RESPA and TILA regulatory requirements relating to compensation paid to parties that act as mortgage brokers (even if they are not called brokers)?

Note: The Bureau has issued a complete exemption to the prohibition on loan originators receiving origination fees or charges from someone other than the consumer where the consumer pays upfront points and fees pursuant to its exemption authority while it scrutinizes several crucial issues relating to the design, operation, and possible effects in a mortgage market undergoing regulatory overhaul of such a restriction.

- Mandatory Arbitration and Financed Credit Insurance

Do your policies and procedures address provisions that:

- Prohibit contracts or agreements from requiring consumers to submit disputes concerning a residential mortgage loan or home equity line of credit to arbitration and do you prohibit applying or interpreting such contracts or agreements to waive federal statutory causes of action?

- Prohibit financing of any premiums or fees for credit insurance or debt cancellation or suspension in connection with a consumer credit transaction secured by a dwelling? (Note: Credit insurance can be paid on a monthly basis and some unemployment insurance is excluded.)

- TILA-RESPA Integrated Disclosures

If you make closed-end credit transaction secured by real property, do your policies and procedures address key provisions that:

- Identify covered transactions?
- Identify transactions where you must continue to use the existing disclosures under TILA and RESPA after the effective date (GFE, initial and final TIL, and the HUD-1)?
- Define pre-consummation and post-consummation disclosure requirements and tolerances?
- Include disclosures required by this rule such as the Loan Estimate, the Closing Disclosure, the post-consummation escrow cancellation notice, (Escrow Closing Notice), and the post-consummation mortgage servicing transfer and partial payment notice?

Loan Estimate
- Outline the six pieces of information that define an "application"?

- Describe what is necessary for a consumer to indicate an intent to proceed?
- Ensure you provide the Loan Estimate no later than 3 business days (days when your offices are open to the public for carrying out substantially all of your business functions) after application and any revised Loan Estimate no later than 4 business days (all calendar days except Sundays and legal public holidays) before consummation (unless the consumer waives the waiting period due to a personal emergency)?
- Make sure the Loan Estimate is correct and that allowable errors are within tolerances?
- No later than three business days after receiving the application, provide a separate list of services for which the consumer may or may not shop and identify at least one provider for each service? (Note: For services for which the consumer may shop, the consumer may choose a different provider than what is on the list).
- Assure that revisions to the Loan Estimate or issuance of a new Loan Estimate comply with the regulatory requirements such as timing?
- Provide disclaimers for written estimates prior to application and for advertisements?
- Charge only permitted fees prior to providing the Loan Estimate?
- Assure that a mortgage broker that provides the Loan Estimate complies with all requirements?

Closing Disclosure

- Assure that the consumer receives the Closing Disclosure at least 3 business days (all calendar days except Sundays and legal public holidays) prior to consummation?
- Provide corrected Closing Disclosures if necessary, that comply with the requirements for timing, corrections due to subsequent changes, and new 3-day waiting period?
- Implement a process for post-consummation review to ensure that you provide corrected Closing Disclosures for non-numerical clerical errors and any estimates above allowable thresholds and that you make refunds to consumers within 60 calendar days of consummation?

2. Do your policies contain all the relevant disclosures, in addition to the Loan Estimate and the Closing Disclosure, required by the new rules?

- Do you use the model disclosure forms and language contained in the regulatory guidance?
  - If not, are your disclosures clearly written in a way that consumers are likely to understand?
  - Are the disclosures presented in a way that is likely to call the consumer's attention to the nature and significance of the information in the notice?

3. Have you established controls to satisfy the timing and method of delivery requirements?

4. Do you retain copies of the disclosures for each of the applicable time periods required by the new rules?

5. Have disclosures been reviewed by compliance and audit?

    - Have the policies been reviewed by the board (or similar oversight functions) and senior management as appropriate, the compliance officer, or legal counsel?
      - Were any concerns identified at this level?
      - If yes, have they been resolved?

6. Do you have testing planned to confirm that your actual practices conform to the policies?

7. What processes do you have in place to ensure that policies are kept current and account for all changes in the regulatory environment?

    - Who is responsible for maintaining content?

8. What steps will you take to ensure that new product development considers new regulatory rules and associated risks?

    - Is the compliance function represented in the new product development process?

9. Do your policies and procedures vary materially by region, by delivery method, or by legal entity?

    - If practices vary:

- Is testing done for each segment?
- Are all policies individually approved?
- What controls are in place to ensure that regulatory updates are accounted for in all policies?

10. Have automated tools been updated to reflect your new policies and procedures?
    - Have they been tested to confirm accuracy?
    - Do they use appropriate data standards and implement the required format?

11. Have you updated your risk assessment to reflect the regulatory changes?
    - Do your policies and procedures define a process for ongoing updates to the risk assessment to account for regulatory changes?

C. Training

1. Have you determined what training needs to be developed?

2. Have you determined who needs training?
    - Does this include your loan officers, processors, closing agents, compliance teams and quality control staff?
    - Does this include monitoring the training your third party service providers are providing for their staff, especially where you may have some responsibility for their actions?

3. Has training been conducted? If so, do you anticipate offering refresher training?

4. Have you considered the following questions in developing training:
    - What information will be covered in the new training?
    - What is the format for training? (Instructor-led, online, etc.)
    - How will training vary based on job duties?
    - How do you document completed training?

- What are the consequences for employees not completing training by the assigned deadline?

- Have the changes to the training program been fully integrated into your full training program and ongoing schedule?

5. How will you roll out the changes to your training program?

    - When will training be completed?

    - Do training timelines allow for enough time for staff to fully understand rule requirements prior to the effective date?

    - Have you done any testing of training program changes?

6. Who is responsible for developing course content?

    - Did you purchase content from an outside vendor?

    - How is senior management involved in developing and approving course content?

    - How did you determine that course content is adequate?

    - What is the process for identifying the need for additional changes?

7. Have you determined what training will be needed to address operational changes?

    - What areas are impacted by the changes?

D. Audit, Compliance Review, Internal Compliance

1. Did audit and compliance specialists review or play a role in developing and implementing your new procedures for complying with the new mortgage rules?

    - If so, did the audit and compliance specialists make any suggestions for process improvement?

    - Are any action items outstanding?

        - How are they being tracked?

- Will enhancements be made prior to the rule effective date?

2. Have audit/compliance review/internal control procedures been updated to reflect the regulatory changes?

    - Have the updated procedures been tested?

    - Has the updated audit/compliance/internal control program been approved by the board (or similar oversight function) and senior management, as appropriate?

    - Have you conducted a pre-exam review to determine level of compliance?

3. Have you conducted any pre-implementation reviews? If so, have you adjusted appropriate elements of your compliance management program where you've identified weaknesses?

E. Complaints

1. What training will the associates that process consumer complaints receive regarding the changes to the mortgage rules?

    - Will applicable training be completed prior to the effective date?

2. Are complaints processed centrally or by individual business lines?

    - If by line of business, how will complaints training vary?

3. Is complaint data analyzed to identify training needs and process breakdowns?

4. How are complaints handled when regulatory violations are noted?

    - Are violations tracked?

    - Is root cause analysis done when violations are noted?

F. Service Provider Management

1. What arrangements, agreements, or contracts exist with vendors and other service providers related to mortgage products or servicing?

    - Do you have changes planned for service provider practices as a result of the new rules?

- Have you evaluated current integrations between your technology platforms and those of your relevant third party providers, such as document generators and settlement service providers to determine what updates are necessary?

- Will your third party service providers deliver compliant application technology releases and/or fully tested process updates in time for the effective dates?

- If your third party service provider is or was not compliant by the effective dates, do you have an alternate plan in place to ensure compliance?

- If no such plan exists, when will such a plan be established?

2. What changes have been made or need to be made to the above arrangements, agreements, or contracts to ensure that service providers comply with new regulations and all legal obligations?

3. Do you review complaints regarding vendor activity for compliance and process concerns?

    - How frequently do you receive this complaint data?

4. Do you receive and review training procedures for third parties related to regulatory requirements?

5. Will you provide training for any third party service providers?

Part III – Frequently Asked Questions

How do I contact the CFPB about the new mortgage rules?
For more information on Regulatory Implementation materials, please contact CFPB_MortgageRulesImplementation@cfpb.gov. Your feedback is crucial to making these materials and this page as helpful as possible.

If, after reviewing the resources on the Regulatory Implementation page and the related regulation(s) and commentary, you have a question regarding regulatory interpretation, please email CFPB_reginquiries@cfpb.gov with your specific question, including reference to the applicable regulation section(s).

For more information regarding using this readiness guide, you may contact the CFPB Office of Supervision by email at CFPB_Supervision@CFPB.gov.

Who must comply with the rule?

Please review the details of the new requirements to determine coverage. You can find additional information about coverage and exemptions found in the TILA-RESPA Integrated Disclosure rule small entity compliance guide.

What does the CFPB expect of institutions when a regulation becomes effective?

The CFPB expects institutions to comply with all relevant provisions by the effective date of the rule. Policies, procedures and training should be updated to ensure that employees fully understand the changes prior to the effective dates.

When will the CFPB start examining for compliance with recent rule changes?

The CFPB will assess policies and procedures in a timely fashion. Transaction testing will not take place until after the effective date of the rule and enough time has passed to allow for an adequate sample of transactions. You should be prepared to discuss your implementation plan and policy changes prior to the effective date of the rule.

Will the CFPB coordinate and communicate supervisory activities with other regulatory agencies?

In accordance with the Dodd-Frank Act and its routine practice, the CFPB will coordinate with other regulators. Regulators will communicate examination plans and findings with each other. When appropriate, the regulators will coordinate examination efforts in order to reduce regulatory burden.

Where can I find CFPB examination procedures and other information?

The examination procedures and links to revised examination procedures that will be incorporated into the full examination manual in the future, can be found on the CFPB website.

http://www.consumerfinance.gov/guidance/supervision/manual/

Where can I find examination procedures for other regulators?

For examination procedures outside the CFPB, you should consult the regulatory agencies' websites.

http://www.occ.gov/topics/examinations/index-examinations.html

http://www.fdic.gov/regulations/

http://www.federalreserve.gov/bankinforeg/default.htm

http://www.ncua.gov/Legal/GuidesEtc/Pages/Examiners-Guide.aspx

http://www.csbs.org

Where do I find additional resources to assist in implementation?

For additional information, you may use the CFPB developed tools and compliance guides. Many of the tools developed by the CFPB can be accessed on our website, http://www.consumerfinance.gov/regulatory-implementation/, or in Part V of this document.

For the TILA-RESPA Integrated Disclosure rule, regulatory support materials can be found at http://www.consumerfinance.gov/regulatory-implementation/tila-respa/. There you will find a Compliance Guide, a Guide to Forms, Integrated loan disclosure forms & samples with blank model loan estimates and closing disclosures showing fields annotated to show rule citations, alternative loan type and Spanish language samples.

Part V – Tools

Below you will find links to further information and CFPB-prepared tools to assist you in complying with the new mortgage rules.

CFPB Regulatory Implementation Webpage

Title XIV Rule Implementation

    Title XIV Mortgage Rules at a Glance

    Ability-to-Repay and Qualified Mortgage Rule Small EntityCompliance Guide

    Ability-to-Repay Requirements with Qualified Mortgages Comparison Chart

    Small Creditor Qualified Mortgages Flowchart

    Mortgage Origination Rules: Transaction Coverage and Exemption Chart

    Loan Originator Compensation Requirements Small Entity Compliance Guide

    TILA Higher-Priced Mortgage Loans (HPML) Escrow Rule Small Entity Compliance Guide

    High-Cost Mortgage and Homeownership Counseling Small Entity Compliance Guide

    ECOA Valuations Rule Small Entity Compliance Guide

    TILA Appraisals for Higher-Priced Mortgage Loans Small Entity Compliance Guide

    TILA and RESPA Servicing Small Entity Compliance Guide

    TILA and RESPA Servicing Coverage Chart

TILA-RESPA Integrated Disclosure Regulatory Implementation

TILA-RESPA Integrated Disclosure Rule Small Entity Compliance Guide

TILA-RESPA Integrated Disclosure Guide to the Loan Estimate and Closing Disclosure forms

Annotated forms for TILA RESPA Integrated Disclosure – Loan Estimate Disclosure

Annotated forms for TILA RESPA Integrated Disclosure – Closing Disclosure

TILA-RESPA Integrated Disclosure timeline example

Recorded webinars on TILA-RESPA Integrated Disclosure rule